E

Typical light bulbs generate disorganized beams of light. Laser lights generate highly organized and focused beams. Light from typical bulbs travels a normal distance, while a laser beam can travel into space. Jim Richards' insights and bits of life history in *Hard Hat Area: Building Biblical Families* make for fascinating reading. But wisely, he turns his thoughts into laser light as he runs them through the filter of God's Word. As I read Richards' latest book, I never was more than a few lines away from the unchanging truth of Scripture. As the culture crumbles under our feet, Richards provides refreshing, straightforward instruction about constructing families on the truth of God's Word.

Richard Ross, PhD., professor of student ministry at Southwestern Baptist Theological Seminary, www.richardaross.com

Families wanting to be successful today are bombarded with too much information from too many unreliable sources. In the midst of all the noise, Jim clearly articulates God's timeless plan for every member of your family. Do what this book says, and then watch God do something amazing in your home!

Barrett & Jenifer Johnson, INFO for Families Cofounders

Hard Hat Area: Building Biblical Families reads like a timeless family coach for every season of life.

Ron Hunter Jr., PhD., cofounder and director of the D6 Conference; author of *The DNA of D6: Building Blocks of Generational Discipleship*

Jim Richards writes with the maturity of a godly father and grandfather and with the skill and precision of a biblical scholar. *Hard Hat Area: Building Biblical Families* helps us to see clearly what the Bible actually says about how we should live as men and women, parents and grandparents, married and single people, when it comes to building families in a God honoring way. Everyone would benefit from this concise and compelling work on effectively navigating the "hard hat area" of home.

Brian Haynes, lead pastor, Bay Area Church
Author of *Shift: What it Takes to Finally Reach Families Today*;
The Legacy Path; and *Relentless Parenting*

Many Christians might characterize our present society as one of spiritual, religious, and moral confusion. Jim Richards clearly spells out God's intentions for the family and the home. This is an excellent read for all members of Christ's body as we plow through the fields of confusion and point our children, families, and congregations to the heavenly Father.

Karen Kennemur, PhD., associate professor of children's ministry
and Bessie Fleming Chair of Childhood Education,
Southwestern Baptist Theological Seminary

DER CONSTRUCTION   ION   UNDER CONSTRU

HARD HAT AREA

BUILDING BIBLICAL FAMILIES

BY JIM RICHARDS

Auxano
PRESS

ISBN: 978-0-578-10954-1

Published by Auxano Press, Traveler's Rest, South Carolina. www.AuxanoPress.com.

Cover design: Lightner Creative, www.LightnerCreative.com

Page Design and Layout: Lightner Creative, www.LightnerCreative.com

Unless otherwise noted, Scripture quotations are taken from the New American Standard Bible® (NASB), Copyright © 1960, 1962, 1963, 1968, 1971, 1972, 1973, 1975, 1977, 1995 by The Lockman Foundation. Used by permission. www.Lockman.org.

Scripture quotations marked NKJV are from the New King James Version®. Copyright © 1982 by Thomas Nelson. Used by permission. All rights reserved.

Scripture quotations marked KJV are from The Authorized (King James) Version. Rights in the Authorized Version in the United Kingdom are vested in the Crown. Reproduced by permission of the Crown's patentee, Cambridge University Press.

Scripture quotations marked CSB have been taken from the Christian Standard Bible®, Copyright © 2017 by Holman Bible Publishers. Used by permission. Christian Standard Bible® and CSB® are federally registered trademarks of Holman Bible Publishers.

Printed in the United States of America
18 19 20 21 22 23—6 5 4 3 2 1

To my three married children and their spouses—

Andy and Rachel Collier
Joe and Rebekah Lightner
Nathan and Whitney Richards

You taught us to live life in a construction zone!

CONTENTS

ACKNOWLEDGMENTS

First and foremost I want to give glory to my Lord and Savior Jesus Christ; His grace is extended to me in eternal life. He has blessed me with the perfect life mate in my wife June. Her faithfulness to our Lord has enabled me to be a better follower of Jesus. She is a tremendous prayer warrior. Without her, a book on the family would be lacking. She was willing to suffer through times when I was unavailable due to my writing, and she never complained. Of course, our children, grandchildren, sons-in-law and daughter-in-law added to the mix. Thank you to my mother and dad who laid the family foundation for me.

Kenneth Priest has been a dear friend and a taskmaster on this project. His belief that I have something to offer to others is a great encouragement. I am in debt to him for this and other books that I have produced. There is no one I admire more.

Randi Kent is my administrative assistant, but she takes on my personal assignments with a gracious, humble spirit. Many thanks to Randi for her help. Lance Crowell and Karen Kennemur put eyes on the writing for grammar and content. These three are work associates who were willing to contribute their private time to making this book possible. Additionally, a special thanks to Lance, who has provided a helpful discussion section at the end of each chapter.

Finally, my pastoral experience was an invaluable resource. Churches I pastored put up with bad sermons as I tried to preach about the family. I am grateful for the families I have watched model biblical principles as they lived in the construction zone.

INTRODUCTION

ENTER THE CONSTRUCTION ZONE

At no point in our culture has the nuclear family been under attack to the extent it is today. Marriage has been redefined by the US Supreme Court to include same-sex couples. Cohabitation has become an accepted practice. Divorce continues to plague our families. Yet the very foundation of our future existence as a society depends on the recovery of a biblical ethic for the family.

Valentine's Day 2018 was marred by a mass shooting at Marjory Stoneman Douglas High School in Parkland, Florida that cost seventeen people their lives. Finger-pointing began immediately. Some blamed law enforcement agencies for their lack of response to warning signs. There were calls for stricter gun laws; others said mental illness played a part in the tragedy. School officials were under scrutiny for their handling of the shooter's disciplinary problems. Finally, someone pointed out that the unfortunate homelife of the former student was the real underlying cause. We may never know all of the factors that contributed to this heartbreaking incident. But we can be certain that a strong homelife can prevent much deviant behavior and provide a nurturing environment. God's plan for the home is the hope for a well-adjusted coming generation.

In Christian circles, marriage and family conferences are abundant. Neophytes write books without life experiences or a scriptural basis. We have one true guide for all things family—the Bible. Scripture gives us the answers to life's hardest questions. Someone said the Bible is the mind of God deposited in a book, delivered to the church to be dispensed in the world. As the mind of God reduced to writing, we hear a clear voice speaking into our current needs.

During the course of this book I will share from life experience. I had a few years away from home as a single person. I know it was a long time ago, but some things never change. My wife and I were a young married couple once. We have three children. All three of them brought different challenges. Now we have grandchildren. As the shadows lengthen on my life, I reflect on my missteps and rejoice in the moments of spiritual clarity. This book will not be infallible, but I hope to point you to some infallible truths found in God's Word.

My wife, June, and I have two girls and a boy. God blessed us with our son when the two girls were fifteen and almost twelve. When our son was about five years old, he had a builder play set. There were audio features on some of the parts. One night my wife heard him stirring in bed so she went to check on him. She stepped on one of the audio buttons, and a voice called out, "Caution, hard hat area!" Of course this woke up everyone. We must be fully awake to the fact that building a home is a construction zone. It will never be complete this side of heaven, but God gives us the blueprints.

Regardless of whether you are single, widowed, an empty nester, or have a house full of kids, home is still where the heart is.

Life's guidebook, the Bible, gives us clear direction in every area of relationships. My desire is to help you build the type of family superstructure that pleases God and produces joy in your life. Only the Lord Jesus Christ can enable us to have the type of home we all desire. By following biblical principles you will be able to have God's best.

I want to announce a disclaimer as I begin the book. I was no perfect parent. Persons who say they have no regrets in life either are lying or have no memory. I messed up big-time over and over. I wish I could relive some of those times when my children were at home. I am grateful that God's grace covers my faults. My wife did most of the heavy lifting. Above all, God's grace allowed us to see all of our children come to know Jesus as their personal Savior. Today all three adult children are serving the Lord with their families. Third John 4 expresses my sentiments, "I have no greater joy than this, to hear of my children walking in the truth." My desire for you is to start where you are, moving your family closer to God's design for your home. Until we see Jesus we will always be in a hard hat area, because building biblical families is a construction zone.

CHAPTER 1

MEN

REAL MEN LOVE JESUS

A popular bumper sticker from a few years ago tried to appeal to the macho side of men. Hollywood has given us a conflicting picture of a real man. Some men are portrayed as animalistic, crude, foul-mouthed and harsh. Others are shown as incompetent, weak, and/or effeminate. How can we tell what a real man is supposed to be? While bumper sticker proclamations may be a little cheesy, the creators of "Real Men Love Jesus" got it right. Anyone can go in the flow with others. It takes a courageous man to identify with the Lord Jesus Christ.

The apostle Paul wrote Holy Spirit inspired eternal truth. God gave us His plan for men. Since creation man has been given the role of priest in the home. As a follower of Jesus, it is incumbent upon us to be God's man in the home. Are you willing to follow His plan? We are going to explore several parts of God's plan for men in the home and along the way find practical application for our lives.

Ephesians 5:23 says, "For the husband is the head of the wife, as Christ also is the head of the church, He Himself being the Savior of the body." Headship is not about rights but responsibilities. A man is to be the leader in the home. Paul used marriage as an analogy of Christ and His church. In this relationship the man is to provide spiritual leadership.

I do not want to be presumptuous that everyone reading this book is a believer. Before you can fulfill God's plan as God's man you have to know Jesus as your personal Lord and Savior. What does it mean to be born again or to be saved? To be a spiritual leader, you begin with your own relationship with God.

Anyone can go in the flow with others. It takes a courageous man to identify with the Lord Jesus Christ.

We all have a problem. It is called sin. God is holy. He has set a standard of conduct in the Ten Commandments that none of us can live up to. Even more revealing is that we cannot live up to the attitudinal expectations of a holy God. Simply not worshipping Him with all of our hearts, minds, and strength is enough to keep us from knowing Him. Basically, there are three ways we sin against God: we break God's law; we do not do what we know we should toward God; we live without submitting to God. The result of sin is spiritual death. Not only are we separated from God, but because of His righteous judgment we will be sent away from God forever to a lake of fire.

But God made a remedy for our sin. Jesus is God in the flesh. He lived a perfect life, which no other person could do. He died on the cross, shedding His blood to pay for our sins. He was resurrected three days later to prove our sins can be forgiven. Now Jesus offers us forgiveness through a personal relationship with Him.

Everyone must respond individually. This is done through repentance and faith. Repentance means we are willing to give control of our lives over to Jesus, letting Him be Lord. To have faith is to believe Jesus will come into our lives and one day He will take us to heaven. There must be a point in time when you consciously commit yourself to the Lord Jesus. If this has never happened to you, you can call on Him now.

Once a man is saved, it is the beginning point of his spiritual leadership. Again, leadership for your wife and family is predicated on your level of spiritual standing. Your family's spiritual health is dependent on your personal growth (2 Peter 3:18). It is a daily walk under the lordship of Jesus that helps us grow spiritually. I confess that I do not live 100 percent of the time under the control of God's Spirit; but when I do, my life is at its best. Confession as a believer mirrors the conversion experience. A daily walk with Jesus is possible by repenting of sin and believing God for forgiveness (1 John 1:9). A person only gets saved once, but a walk with Jesus is a continual renewal each day.

Humility is the key to leadership. James 4 says, "God is opposed to the proud, but gives grace to the humble"; and, "Humble yourselves in the presence of the Lord, and He will exalt you" (verses 6, 10). Your personal, basic discipleship provides a platform for you to build a more spiritual life. Daily Bible study and prayer are essential. Sharing your faith will put you in the top 3 percent of evangelical Christians. Regular community with the church is essential. Giving monetarily and giving of your own self will enrich your life.

Once you settle your walk with God, you can turn your attention to your family. Spiritual leadership begins in your heart and pours over into your home. As the spiritual leader, you would be the one to read Scripture, pray, and take ownership of showing your wife and children how to follow Jesus. You are to be the leader by setting the spiritual climate in your home.

First Corinthians 16:13 says to "act like men." Making right choices in front of your wife and children sets the direction for your family. What you watch on television, how you spend your leisure time, and how you interact with others all show a pattern for your children to follow. There are five questions you can ask yourself when engaging the world system.

1. *Will I have more power as a Christian?* First Corinthians 6:12 answers the question. We are to walk with Jesus in such a way that nothing can gain control over us. Substance abuse begins with no intention to become addicted.

2. *Will my activity bring glory to God?* Everything we do should be harmless to our witness. We are to glorify God in every area of our lives (1 Corinthians 10:31).

3. *What type of atmosphere will I be in, spiritual or carnal?* First Thessalonians 5 says, "Abstain from all appearance of evil" (verse 22 KJV). If a place or activity has a connotation of evil, stay away from it. This is to be done not in a sanctimonious way but with a gracious spirit. It is better to be safe than sorry you were there.

4. *Will I cause someone to sin or stumble in their spiritual walk?* Romans 14:13 pleads with us to consider the spiritual welfare of others rather than testing the limits of our liberties in Christ. This is especially applicable to children. They will mimic our actions, whether good or bad.

5. *Who are my most intimate friends?* We are not to live in monasteries or avoid people who need Jesus, but we are to cultivate our deepest friendships with those who know Him. My granddad used to say that if you

lie down with a dog that has ticks, you will get up with some on you. Scripture bears out that axiom in 1 Corinthians 15:33.

Ephesians 5:25-33 declares unequivocally that a man is to be a lover in the home. A lover is not a bed-hopping womanizer. Being a lover is taking the principles of love from Jesus' relationship with the church and applying it to your wife. Remember, the husband/wife relationship is an analogy of Christ's relationship with the church. This section of Scripture puts the highest demands on a man. Generally, women are more emotionally in tune, and generally, men are more logical in their approach to life's situations. This poses a problem for the average man to be what God wants him to be. Expressing love is hard work for most men. A husband will show his love for his wife in a number of ways.

In Ephesians 5:25 a husband is to express *agape* love. This is a Godlike love. How much did Jesus love the church? He went to the cross to show it. Men are rarely called upon to put their lives in danger to show love to their wives. Men are not necessarily called upon to die for their wives. However, men are expected to live for their wives' betterment in every way. Men are to be the ones who give. This means giving up rights to bless the other.

Verses 26 and 27 indicate the attention necessary to have a good relationship in a marriage. Jesus interacts with the church on a regular basis. The "washing of water with the word" is the continual care of the Holy Spirit applying the scriptures to our lives. Constant attention must be given to the needs of the wife. Most women spell love T-I-M-E. Time conveys security and reassurance. Time investment is the only way to adequately build a relationship. Gary Chapman, in his book *The Five Love Languages*, lists these ways to express love: Gifts, Quality Time, Words of Affirmation, Acts of Service, and Physical Touch.[1]

A husband is to express exclusive love to his wife (verses 28-31). You are to have eyes only for each other. You should have only one wife (Exodus 20:14). Flirting has no place in the life of the believer (Proverbs 6:27), and there is no room for fantasizing. Pornography is at an epidemic proportion among men, and men within the church are not immune. Pornography has been called the "empty embrace"—it is one of the most hollow, yet destructive, sexual practices. You are to be a one-woman man. Being one flesh is more than a sexual expression; you become one with your wife. Whatever happens to you happens to her. The emotional and spiritual meshing is at a higher level than the physical union. This is why adultery is a sin against your own body (1 Corinthians 6:18).

Love must prevail even in times of disagreement and dishonor. The word *divorce* should not be in the Christian's vocabulary. Imperfections allow us to see God's work in our lives. Our responsibility as men means we are to extend grace to our wives even if it means to be like Hosea, who had to woo his prostitute wife back to himself. In less extreme cases, opposing wills find peace in prayer and at the foot of the cross. Personality differences may be heavenly sandpaper rubbing off the rough edges in our lives.

The book of Ephesians also addresses God's man in the home as it relates to children. For those with children or grandchildren, or who will one day have children, God's plan is for you to be a life shaper (Ephesians 6:4). Scripture refers to the father as the leader and lover in the home. When we look at children, we find every child has three basic needs: testimony, touch, and talk. Spiritual growth in children is supplied by having a dad in the home. Ultimately, the child must make the spiritual decision that will frame his or her life. Dads can have a strong influence for good and God.

Give your children a testimony. "Do not provoke" them, but live the gospel in front of them. Let them hear you admit when you are wrong. Let them see you humble yourself before the Lord. "Do as I say and not as I do" will not work. Hypocrisy will only alienate you from your kids.

Touch your children. Training is instruction by discipline.

Most kids just need a pat on the back. Some need it a little lower and a little harder than others. Hebrews 12:5-11 shows how our loving heavenly Father corrects us so we can experience His best for us. Child abuse is an intolerable act. Discipline should never be done in anger, but the proper use of corporal punishment is a way to show correction. Loving discipline is affirmed throughout the scriptures (Proverbs 13:24; 19:18; 22:15; 29:15).

Talk to your children. To "admonish" children is to use words to train them. Someone reported that the average dad spends three minutes in conversation with his child. Interaction is to be done not just at a time of correction but in casual conversation. Dads can begin the relationship building process by taking time to talk.

God's plan for God's man in the home comes back to Joshua's declaration, "As for me and my house we will serve the LORD," (Joshua 24:15). It is the man who declares he will set the standard for God in his life, with his wife and in his home.

---

1 Gary Chapman, *The Five Love Languages* (Chicago: Northfield Publishing, 2015).

FOR FURTHER STUDY AND DISCUSSION

1. Have you ever personally trusted Jesus Christ to save you from your sins?

2. Take time today to make sure that the families in your church have a personal testimony about how God has saved them. Encourage parents to share their story of faith with their spouse and children.

3. What are some areas of pride that we struggle with in our lives?

4. How can you take steps to be humble before God and around those you love?

5. What are some of the attributes of a real man of God?

6. Love is such a misunderstood and misused term in our world, how can we as men demonstrate God's love in the places he has planted us? Home? Church? Work? Community?

CHAPTER 2

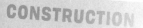

WOMEN

YOU'VE COME A LONG WAY, BABY!

his was the promotional slogan for the first cigarette designed exclusively for women. The year was 1968 at the beginning of the so-called Women's Liberation Movement. Ironically, the cigarette known as Virginia Slims was the last of its kind to have a commercial aired on television.[1] Thus, we have Exhibit A in the case against the culture trying to set the course for women's advancement.

Traditional roles for women have shifted more in my lifetime than since the beginning of time. Most changes have been healthy and positive. Society has long been influenced by women, but only recently has the influence been as direct. The home has always been the center of most activity for the woman. Shifting patterns indicate less time being spent in the home by women than ever before. In relationship to the Christian community, the role of women in ministry provokes great controversy. It is my intention to avoid traditional concepts, prejudicial attitudes, and personal opinions as we examine the role of women. The Bible gives us the basis for our beliefs.

The Bible is the inerrant, infallible, God-breathed instruction book for our actions. Jesus said the Word of God is the measuring stick for time and eternity (John 12:48). The Bible provides us with all the necessary information to draw our conclusions (2 Timothy 3:16-17). Whether by precept or principle the Word of God instructs us.

I have a personal interest in the role of women. I have a wife, two daughters, and two granddaughters. Any good parent wants what is best for his or her child. I want the women in my life to excel in every area. God created woman and gave her a particular place in the order of existence. He wants every woman to fulfill her divinely directed potential. There are three areas of involvement for women that we shall explore.

Society has long been influenced by women, but only recently has the influence been as direct.

The role of women should be recognized beginning with their contributions to society. Women have taken to the forefront as champions of social causes. American history shows a long-standing advocacy of cultural betterment. Mary Lyons pushed for women's higher education. Dorthea Dix fought for the care of those suffering from mental disorders. Elizabeth Blackwell was the first female medical doctor. In less than one hundred years from the passage of the Nineteenth Amendment guaranteeing women the right to vote, women are senators, governors, and have run for president. There is nothing in the scriptures that prohibits a woman from leadership in government, industry, commerce, or management.

Miriam assisted Moses in the direction of three million Jews

(Exodus 15:19-20; Micah 6:4). Deborah was the head of state during Israel's period of the judges (Judges 4). The Queen of Sheba is mentioned favorably in 1 Kings 10. Many biblical examples can be given where women participated in decision-making, issued instructions, and directed the course of history.

A woman can be active in the home and society. Proverbs 31 is the quintessential chapter about the most admired woman. The passage shows a woman as an industrialist, manager, realtor, horticulturist, shopper, philanthropist, and seamstress. Never let it be said that the Bible teaches a woman should never work outside the home. Society is greatly improved by the participation of women.

My mother was a nurse. She excelled academically. She managed finances incredibly well. She supervised others. Her work required her to be away from home at various times. However, she never forgot her highest calling—our home.

The woman is the heart of the home. God's design for a home includes a wife and/or mother. It is vital to acknowledge that God's view about the home is more important than feminists, chauvinists, or those who considered themselves more enlightened. God is a God of order. He established an order in the home: "Wives, be subject to your own husbands, as to the Lord. For the husband is the head of the wife, as Christ also is the head of the church, He Himself being the Savior of the body. But as the church is subject to Christ, so also the wives ought to be to their husbands in everything," and "the wife must see to it that she respects her husband" (Ephesians 5:22-24, 33).

Women have an invaluable place in God's work. Yet biblical truth is seen as controversial. There are two insights about women in the Ephesians text. Women have an assigned role found in verses 22 and 24. *Hupotasso* is the Greek word translated "submit" or "subject." It is a military term meaning "to arrange in order." It presents the picture of soldiers being arranged under one another in rank. First Corinthians 15:28 says that the Son in His earthly ministry was subject to the

Father. Jesus is not a second-rate person in the Godhead. Jesus is just as much God as the Father. The Holy Spirit is just as much God as Jesus. However, the Holy Spirit is not to promote Himself but glorify Jesus (John 15:26). Each person of the Godhead has a specific role. By a woman fulfilling God's role assignment, she is at her best. No promotion exists above God's plan for you.

Paul, writing to the troubled Corinthian church, illustrates God's order in the home by using an example about hair length in the worship setting (1 Corinthians 11:3-16). He clearly states that hairstyles in worship should not divide the church; he does not negate the truth he is presenting. Verse 3 is the crux of the matter, "But I want you to understand that Christ is the head of every man, and the man is the head of woman, and God is the head of Christ." Ladies, headship is not some power position men have. Headship is a role of responsibility. The man is to be the spiritual leader and the example of love in the home, as we discussed in chapter 1 of this book, which is addressed to men.

Ephesians 5:33 uses the word "respect" to describe the attitude a wife is to have toward her husband. It comes from the Greek word *phobus* from which we get our English word "fear." The fear referred to is a "dread of displeasing." A person in love desires and works for the best of the other. When the man is fulfilling his role, and the woman is fulfilling hers, those observing see a beautiful picture of Christ and the church.

First Peter 3:1-6, shows the importance of a woman's role in the home as it relates particularly to an unsaved husband. I address this in my book *Encouraging Words for Difficult Days*: "Speaking directly to women whose husbands were unbelievers, Peter tells the wives that they could hold the key to their husband's salvation. Peter was calling for more than outward acts of obedience but a holy lifestyle before God with a sweet spirit. A woman's godly behavior is the primary influence on unbelieving husbands."[2]

Proverbs 31:10-31 gives the example of the most "excellent" of women. The original intended audience was not young women, but young men. The New American Commentary states that the message of the poem describes the kind of wife a man needs in order to be successful in life.[3]

King Lemuel is receiving direction from his mother beginning in the first verse. Lemuel means "God-ward."[4] He is told what it will take for him to be a good king in verses 1-9. She then turns her instruction to him about finding the right wife. The last influence a parent hopes to have in a child's life is the choice of their life mate. A parent may not know who he or she should be, but the parent can usually determine who he or she should not be.

I used this text when I preached my mother's funeral. The passage provides testimony to the type of person my wife is. I have been blessed by God's grace, because a godly woman surpasses any earthly value. A woman is the heart of the home.

Proverbs 31:23 says that a virtuous woman may be the central contribution to a man's status. A man has confidence in his wife when she lives in a holy and pure way. My wife's prayer life, godly lifestyle, and unqualified support have enabled me to pursue God's will without any encumbrances from her. I have failed God many times, but it was never because she contributed to that failure.

The description given of the excellent wife reveals an entrepreneurial working mom. Many mothers in biblical times worked outside the home. Even though outside work is permitted, and even commended, the first priority is the home. The expectation for women in today's world is extremely demanding. There is no greater joy than to fulfill God's expectations in the home. There is no greater contribution than to invest in the life of a child. My mother's lips have fallen silent. I can no longer hear her counsel in my ear, but deep within my heart are the counsels of a thousand nights when she read the Word of God to me.

Maybe you did not have a mother like mine. Maybe you feel that you do not relate to some of the things in Proverbs 31. God is able to fill those voids. Jesus is the great equalizer. If your childhood home was not a biblical example, you can make yours one.

You can help someone else to make their home godly. The truth of God's Word brings peace to any situation.

Women, you are free to reach any height in society. Just keep in mind your role in the home. God made each woman for a specific purpose. You are not second-class because you are not in the same place or role as a man. Every person, male or female, does the best for him- or herself and for God's glory when the person fulfills his or her divinely designed role.

1 "The Banning of Cigarette Commercials From TV (and Other Dangerous Products)," Soapboxie, updated October 8, 2016, https://soapboxie.com/social-issues/The-Banning-of-Cigarette-Commercials-and-Other-Dangerous-Products.

2 Jim Richards, *Encouraging Words for Difficult Days: 1 & 2 Peter and Jude* (Tigerville, SC: Auxano Press, 2017), 40.

3 Duane A. Garrett, *Proverbs, Ecclesiastes, Song of Songs*, vol. 14, The New American Commentary (Nashville: Broadman and Holman Publishers, 1993), 245-250.

4 Ibid.

FOR FURTHER STUDY AND DISCUSSION

1. Why are roles in the home so essential?

2. Reflect on how the Bible has been encouraging toward women in society.

3. Read Proverbs 31. Which attributes of the woman of God stick out to you?

4. What are some ways that a wife can respect her husband?

5. Husbands, what can you do to honor your wife as a Proverbs 31 woman?

6. How can parents encourage today's girls to grow up to embrace their role in the home and their opportunities in society?

CHAPTER 3

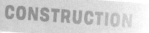

FAMILY

WHO WILL YOU PUT ON THE ALTAR?

O n our honeymoon night June and I started a time of family worship. We prayed and read Scripture together. Since that time, there have been fewer than a dozen times we have pillowed our heads at night that we did not have a family worship time. When our children came along, we continued the practice. In those days family worship was called, "the family altar." This was an appropriate term because there were times when we wanted to offer up one of our children. Seriously, it was a challenge to get a two-year-old to sit still for a Bible reading. In the beginning of our child-rearing all we had was a King James Version Bible. Our girls had to learn the "thee's" and "thou's." We used the large coffee-table type family Bible. By the time our son came along, we were able to use illustrated children's Bibles and even video helps. Now that June and I are empty nesters, we still have our family worship. God is gracious to let us see our married children carrying on the practice of family worship.

Family worship is outlined in Deuteronomy 6. This passage of Scripture is a mountain peak in the Old Testament. The Ten Commandments is the Law of Moses in a condensed form, and the *Shema* is the Ten Commandments condensed into a few lines. It teaches there is the one and only God and to obey Him is to love Him.

Other than divine providence, family worship is what allowed the Jewish people to be sustained throughout the centuries. Without a homeland for almost two millennia, the family unit perpetuated the religious teachings of the preceding generations. The basic element of the teachings is what the Jews call the Shema. *Shema*, or "Hear," is the first word in verse 4. Jesus used the Shema to answer a question about the greatest commandment. The Shema continues to be recited daily by the devout Jew. It was used to regularly and routinely instruct the family about loving God. Instilling spiritual truth begins in the home. The responsibility of discipleship was centered in the Jewish home, not the synagogue or temple.

God gives clear principles for family worship in Deuteronomy 6:4-9.

> "Hear, O Israel! The LORD is our God, the LORD is one! You shall love the LORD your God with all your heart and with all your soul and with all your might. These words, which I am commanding you today, shall be on your heart. You shall teach them diligently to your sons and shall talk of them when you sit in your house and when you walk by the way and when you lie down and when you rise up. You shall bind them as a sign on your hand and they shall be as frontals on your forehead. You shall write them on the doorposts of your house and on your gates."

Do you want your home transformed? Any family can experience change. There are no magical formulas or easy fixes, but you can see God begin to work in your home. It is easier to start at the first of a marriage relationship, but you can start practicing family worship at any point. Praying over a newborn, reading and singing to a preschooler, teaching a child, or instructing a teenager will impact their lives for time and eternity.

Deuteronomy 6:7 points out the importance of teaching God's Word. This is the basis of all truth (2 Timothy 3:16) and the first principle of family worship. We have nowhere else to turn when we want absolute truth. Genesis 1 gives no argument for God's existence. It declares that the true and living God created all things. The cause of sin, suffering, and death is explained in chapter 3. God's remedy is promised too. All of life's perplexing issues are addressed in the Bible. Every page tells us about God's love. The recurring theme is that God came in the flesh to redeem us for His glory.

Moral values are an outgrowth of knowing God. Since God is holy, He calls for us to be like Him. Although we will never reach perfection this side of heaven, we can have the power of God's indwelling Spirit, enabling us to live far beyond our ability. In every area of life His design is not just a good one or the best one. It is the only one.

In many situations dads have abdicated the role of spiritual leader in the home. Thank God for wives and mothers who lead. God's Plan A, though, is for the husband/father to lead the home. Ephesians 5:25, 28-31 show the spiritual role of the husband in the home. This leadership has to be more than prayer at a meal. A lifestyle of a man honoring his wife illustrates Jesus' love for the church. Ephesians 6:4 is a direct command for the father to be integrally engaged in the life of his child. Statistics bear out that absentee fathers are a plague on society.[1] Single mothers do double duty when the father absolves himself of the God-given assignment of being a dad.

There is no substitute for a husband taking his wife's hand to lead in prayer. Nothing can take the place of a dad reading God's Word to his children. Living out the teachings of Jesus daily before his children is an invaluable investment. Even when failing (there are no perfect dads) a dad can show how God's grace can cover his sin. Being honest with his wife or children about his error will reinforce what he has been teaching. Transparency as a dad supersedes anything we could do by mere rule keeping.

The teacher who teaches, teaches best by example. Being the head of the house is not an authority like a stick to wield but a responsibility to live. A wife and mother teaches from the moment of her child's birth until her last breath. Using the Word of God, she instills eternal values. Proverbs 31 tells of the influence of a godly mother. Family members praise the woman who guides them in truth. The most enduring quality in the life of children is her relationship with the Lord. No greater praise can be given—that a mother taught her children the things of God. Acts 16:14-15 tells of a mother who trusted Jesus as her Savior. There is no mention of her husband; she may have been a single mom. Those in her household were saved through her decision to follow Jesus. It takes a personal relationship with Jesus Christ to lay the foundation of an enduring heritage. My mother prayed over me to be saved. She would not let me go to hell. She later prayed for me as I sought to live for the Lord. Because of her witness, I am writing these words. I dare to think what would have happened to me without a faithful mother teaching me the way of God.

It takes a personal relationship with Jesus Christ to lay the foundation of an enduring heritage.

If we do not instruct our children about a relationship with Jesus, the culture will indoctrinate them in the empty religion of humanism. Do your part, and leave the rest with the Lord. The family must find time to share and connect.

The second principle is to talk to family members with a spiritual intentionality. Conversations guided by biblical principles will build up your relationships at home. There is no substitute for interaction on a continual basis with the ones you love. Romans 15:7 tells us to accept one another as Jesus accepted us. We are all flawed people. Often we give friends greater latitude than our family members. Use words to encourage family members. Ridicule can abuse the spirit even when the body is untouched. Use scriptural truth to relate to one another.

The third principle is disciplining to serve. Can you imagine having frontlets between your eyes? The first image that comes to my mind is discipline. It would take discipline to wear the frontlets. Modern practicing Jews use phylacteries similar to those in ancient times. They bind leather boxes on their arms and around their heads. The Shema is inside the boxes. These articles identify Jews who wear them as members of the covenant community. Moses' instruction was a metaphor for expressing your love for God. The home is designed to teach discipline. While we don't wear phylacteries, we show our love for God by being disciplined to serve others.

Our family worship is more than singing, praying, and teaching. Family worship should culminate in touching others. Ministering to neighbors, classmates, and work associates should be the result of family worship. A Christian family is to be a witness. Sharing the love of Jesus with those outside our circle will become a natural overflow. We are to let the truth of the love of God permeate every area of our lives.

We are to be different, not a weird different but different in worldview. The church, the school, or the government are not tasked with training a child in the ways of God. It is incumbent on dads and moms to teach spiritual disciplines. Our culture has little hope because our homes have little holiness. We want public holiness legislated, but we practice little private holiness.

When Jews write the Shema on their doorposts, it lets

everyone know the home is dedicated to Jehovah. Many Israelis have a receptacle at their door called a Mezuzah with scriptures inside. A rabbi explained the symbolism of the Mezuzah one time as they want the internal world to reflect godly ideals, to protect against the outside world at the point of interface: the doorway. This means monitoring the contents of books, games, and video to which children are exposed.

The primary purpose in family worship is deeply planting a love for our Savior within our hearts. The lordship of Jesus is evident in a home when Jesus is worshipped. Parents must protect their children from as much evil as possible. Parents are then to prepare their children to face evil with the power of the gospel. Families will find their strength not in sports, money, education, activities, or even the church. Jesus must be Lord in the home!

Some Christians want prayer in the classroom, yet they don't pray in their living room. Some want godliness in the White House, yet they live without God in their own house. Families want economic security, but they are not concerned about eternal security. Some homes contain all Christians, but it is not a Christian home. God can make a home different by the power of Jesus Christ. It starts with a parent's decision to follow Jesus. Jesus can transform a life and provide a change agent for your home.

Are you willing to make Jesus Lord of your family? The answer lies in the question, who will you put on the altar? Romans 12:1-2 tells us that we are a living sacrifice. Dads, moms, and other family members must climb upon the altar every day. When we make this a conscious decision, we will see the power of God displayed in our homes.

---

1 "The Proof Is In: Father Absence Harms Children," National Fatherhood Initiative, accessed May 2, 2018, https://www.fatherhood.org/father-absence-statistic.

FOR FURTHER STUDY AND DISCUSSION

1. Do the families in your church have a family altar?

2. What are some ways that families can initiate family worship in the home?

3. Read Deuteronomy 6:4-9, and determine a few times during the day that families can talk about the truths of God's Word.

4. As a family, talk about the evils in the world that work to destroy the family.

5. How can your family serve other families in your community?

CHAPTER 4

CHILDREN

JESUS LOVES THE LITTLE CHILDREN

hild abuse is a terrible, recurring atrocity. Child pornography, sex slavery, and physical abuse are an ugly part of our national story. Children die at the hands of sexual perverts. Child abuse is reported every ten seconds.[1] Overseas the situation is worse. Children in China and India experience indescribable conditions.

Children in the ancient world had no rights. Childhood was an extremely demeaning time. Jesus taught that children were important. One of His more celebrated encounters with children is recorded in Mark's gospel. Jesus used this opportunity to teach a lesson about the kingdom of God. He also affirmed the value of children. Mark's account allows us to see the heart of Jesus through His interaction with children.

Then they brought little children to Him, that He might touch them; but the disciples rebuked those who brought them. But when Jesus saw it, He was greatly displeased and said to them, "Let the little children come to Me, and do not forbid them; for of such is the kingdom of God. Assuredly, I say to you, whoever does not receive the kingdom of God as a little child will by no means enter it." And He took them up in His arms, put His hands on them and blessed them. (Mark 10:13-16 NKJV)

There are four participants in this Kingdom illustration. The first participants are the caring people in the children's lives (verse 13a). We do not know if these were parents, teachers, or some concerned person. We do know that they were on a mission. The touch of Jesus usually meant healing or deliverance. Here, it meant blessing. These guardians were determined to bring the children to Jesus, and they would not be dissuaded. Regardless of the obstacles, a parent has to be committed to introducing his or her child to Jesus. This means an intentional systematic presentation of the gospel facts. Jesus must become real to the child for the child to have a personal relationship with Him as Lord and Savior. The guardians in the story had one driving force: to get their children to Jesus. When a parent has the desire for Jesus to "touch" their children, the parent has to be willing to do whatever is necessary to get them to Him. We cannot make people come to Christ, but we can make it conducive for them.

> *When a parent has the desire for Jesus to "touch" their children, the parent has to be willing to do whatever is necessary to get them to Him.*

One of my first full-time church staff positions was an assistant bus ministry director and children's church pastor. Literally, scores of buses left the church on

Sunday to pick up children who were generally unaccustomed to attending church. My congregation consisted of several hundred children in a gymnasium. These children rarely had anyone to care for them. Their parents may have seen our ministry as an opportunity to get away from their kids for a couple of hours. We saw it as the privilege to share the life-changing message of Jesus with them. Every parent, childcare worker, or those involved in children's ministry participated in getting the children to Jesus. Christian parents have the awesome thrill of being on the inside to bring their children to Him.

The second participants are the critics (verse 13b). The disciples were supposed to be learning Jesus' heart. They were trying to protect Him from those they considered to be unimportant. Unfortunately, the very ones who are supposed to lead people to Jesus are often the stumbling blocks. The church, parents, or other influential people can hinder children and adults from reaching Christ. Sometimes Jesus' followers get their priorities out of order. Failing to see the value of people in general, and children in particular, can cause us to be far from Jesus' heart.

Shortly after answering God's call to the preaching ministry, I was at a church where I asked the pastor about starting a ministry to bring unchurched kids to church. He said they would be disruptive. He said they would soil the carpet. He said they would not be able to produce enough revenue to pay for any outreach we did for them. Needless to say, we did not have a children's outreach. Jesus has some choice words for those who take that position. Matthew 18:10 says, "See that you do not despise one of these little ones, for I say to you that their angels in heaven continually see the face of My Father who is in heaven."

Jesus said those who disregard the spiritual care of children should face a harsh penalty. He said, "But whoever causes one of these little ones who believe in Me to stumble, it is better for him to have a heavy millstone hung around his neck, and to be drowned in the depth of the sea" (verse 6). A millstone could weigh up to

33

one ton. This meant a person mistreating a child should expect judgment. Care should be taken in dealing with children or anyone for that matter in the spiritual realm. An act or an attitude can "hinder" someone from coming to Jesus. My good friend, Joe Senn, who is in heaven now, once served as my student minister. Even though a believer, he used alcohol for a number of years before getting his heart right with the Lord. After answering God's call on his life for vocational ministry, he continued to drink beer occasionally. A few months into his ministry, he was having a beer at a pizza restaurant with his family. He saw one of his students come in to eat. He told me he wanted to hide under the table. He was greatly concerned that his liberty in Christ would destroy one of his "children." He never took another drink. May God help us to be sensitive to our testimony in front of everyone, but especially our children.

The children in this story from Mark's gospel are the focal point (verses 14b-15). The age of the children is not revealed. The Greek word used in this text could mean anything from an infant to twelve years of age. Some use the passage to teach infant baptism, but the text only supports a visit with Jesus. Here the children are coming to Jesus. We can even project with good logic that the children approached Jesus by their own volition. Yet children are to be led to Jesus as well, and parents are in the unique position to influence them that direction. Proverbs tells us:

> Buy—and do not sell—truth,
> wisdom, instruction, and understanding.
> The father of a righteous son will rejoice greatly,
> and one who fathers a wise son will delight in him.
> Let your father and mother have joy,
> and let her who gave birth to you rejoice. (23:23-26 CSB)

I have had parents tell me that they did not want to influence their children about a decision to follow Jesus. They wanted their children to be old enough to make their own choices. If we used the same rationale about bringing our children to Jesus that we do with hygiene, preteen boys would not take a bath. As parents we are to show them the way to Jesus.

The influence of a parent is huge. I witnessed to a man who refused to accept Jesus. I turned to his young teenage son and asked him if he would like to accept Jesus. He said, "When my dad does, I will." As far as I know, neither of them ever came to Christ.

Proverbs 22:6 says, "Train up a child in the way he should go, / Even when he is old he will not depart from it." I heard a great preacher say that this statement is a proverb not a promise. Parents do have a tremendous responsibility to bring their children to Jesus, but the child or teen must genuinely make his or her own decision to receive Jesus as Lord and Savior. While it is incumbent on parents to do everything they can to bring their child to Jesus, parents cannot be held accountable for a child's rebellion or rejection.

Christian parents have the awesome thrill of being on the inside to bring their children to Jesus.

Mark 10:15 describes everyone's status before Jesus: "Whoever does not receive the kingdom of God like a child will not enter it at all." We are all helpless in our own abilities. As the book of Isaiah says, "A little child shall lead them" (11:6 NKJV). Children in their natural state show us how we are to come to Jesus in our spiritual approach. Those who enter the Kingdom do so weak, dependent, insignificant, and trusting.

The fourth participant in this setting is Christ Himself. In verse 14a, the word used for "displeased" conveys the meaning of deep grief. Jesus was sorrowed that the disciples missed His heart's desire. He wanted to be with the children. He wanted the humble, the lowly, the undesirable, the ignored, and the outcast in His presence. In this story Jesus gives the children what all of us need: time, touch, and truth. These qualities are required of a good father. Paul, in his household code, says, "Fathers, do not provoke your children to anger, but bring them up in the discipline and instruction of the Lord" (Ephesians 6:4).

While there should be quality time investment with children, the children notice the *quantity* of time. Just being there counts greatly to a child. While some parents have to be away from their families for an extended period, nothing fills the void of absence like the person's presence at a ballgame, concert, or the evening dinner table.

Something that is missing in most homes today is corporal punishment. My parents believed in major punishment, not just corporal. Actually, I must confess that I did not receive as much as I deserved. Paul used the word "instruction." This touch can be a swat or a hug. Both are needed. Of course, the truth has to be lived out as well as preached. Children in the family know what takes place behind closed doors. They see right through inconsistency. Being transparent with a child is the willingness to admit failure and sin. Spiritual truth will win out.

Jesus had a special place in His heart for children. He raised them from the dead. He healed them, talked to them, and taught with them as an example. Jesus' love expressed on the cross is for all adults and children alike. We become the children of God through the new birth. Anyone at any age can experience the saving grace of the Lord Jesus. My wife tells about the moment she came to Jesus. It was on Mother's Day when she was nine years old. She does not remember the sermon or the preacher's name, but she remembers how she wanted Jesus as her Savior. She trusted Him to forgive her of her sins. From that moment on, she never wavered in her faith. She is a wife, mother, and grandmother. She has served as piano player, children's church leader, nursery worker, Bible teacher, church planter partner, and minister's wife. A little girl who came to Christ has a testimony of living for Jesus for more than a half century. This is why we must bring children to Jesus.

1 "Child Abuse Statistics and Facts," Childhelp, accessed May 2, 2018, https://www.childhelp.org/child-abuse-statistics/.

FOR FURTHER STUDY AND DISCUSSION

1. Jesus made it a priority to demonstrate his love for children, the marginalized in the culture. How can we as a church family prioritize children?

2. God has given us the mandate to care for those who cannot take care of themselves. As a church how are you ministering to orphans and children in need?

3. How can we help parents understand how to share the good news of Jesus with their children?

4. In what ways can you help the families in your church work to prioritize time together instead of being distracted by the busyness of life?

5. Pray for the families in your church that they would raise the next generation to know and love Jesus.

6. Moms and Dads, write out the spiritual goals you have for your children in life.

CHAPTER 5

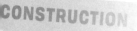

RAISING KIDS

Allowing biblical principles to be the prevailing standard of conduct in the home will change our culture. As parents, we desire the best for our children. Everyone agrees that children should be loved. The problem we have is that although everyone uses the same vocabulary, different groups use a different dictionary. How do we love in the home? How is it shown?

Paul and Peter include "household" codes in some of their letters. These are sections in the correspondence that address the roles, rights, and responsibilities in the home. Just before the quintessential outline of homelife in Ephesians 5:22–6:4 Paul gives a warning about the reality that time is a nonrenewable resource. He said we must use it wisely, "making the most of your time" (Ephesians 5:16). Showing love to our children is often measured in time. As I said earlier, love can be spelled T-I-M-E.

Showing affection in the proper way will help our children know they are loved. Children pay attention to how their dad treats their mom. Little girls will expect their husband to treat them similarly. A little boy will pick up on how to treat his prospective wife. Affection is displayed with a loving touch. Jesus did that when He prayed for the children who came to Him. "Then some children were brought to Him so that He might lay His hands on them and pray" (Matthew 19:13). My son was a college football player who even went to an NFL camp. He played on the offensive line. Even though he was much bigger than me, he never shied away from my hugs and kisses. As a grown man he welcomes my affection. My daughters were always welcome in my lap. I kissed and hugged them. I still do even though they have children of their own.

Frederick of Barbarossa was the first Holy Roman emperor. He lived in the twelfth century. Legend has it that he experimented with infants to see what language they would speak if no one talked to them. Would they speak Hebrew or speak their parents' language? Instead, as the account goes, they were mute. This cruel experiment proved more than a scientific fact. The children needed human interaction to thrive. Our children need communication with parents early and often.

Children also need discipline. Ephesians 6:4 says, "Fathers, do not provoke your children to anger, but bring them up in the discipline and instruction of the Lord." The best teacher is *example*. The old adage, "Do as I say, not as I do" never works. As parents set the proper example before their children, there are times when instruction includes discipline. My parents told me they were disciplining me because they loved me. If my parents had loved me any more than they did, I don't know if I would have survived. Truthfully, I did not get as much correction as I deserved. The Bible says a loving father corrects his children.

It is for discipline that you endure; God deals with you as with sons; for what son is there whom his father does not discipline? But if you are without discipline, of which all have become partakers, then you are illegitimate children and not sons. Furthermore, we had earthly fathers to discipline us, and we respected them; shall we not much rather be subject to the Father of spirits, and live? For they disciplined us for a short time as seemed best to them, but He disciplines us for our good, so that we may share His holiness. All discipline for the moment seems not to be joyful, but sorrowful; yet to those who have trained by it, afterwards it yields the peaceful fruit of righteousness. (Hebrews 12:7-11)

Because of the awareness of child abuse parents have shied away from physical correction. Parents can lose their rights to their children in some states under certain rules governing physical correction. Abuse is a horrific practice, but corporal punishment, properly applied, is not child abuse. Humankind is not basically good. Because of the first parents we come into this world with a selfish desire to do what we want to do with our lives. This sin nature makes us basically bad. Children do not have to be taught how to be bad; they have to be taught how to be good and godly. We are born with a nature to go against God. Proverbs 22:15 says, "Foolishness is bound up in the heart of a child; / The rod of discipline will remove it far from him." Is it still appropriate to spank children? The teaching principles in Scripture have not changed. A child needs to know why he or she is being spanked. Proverbs 29:15 includes both elements in correction: "The rod and reproof give wisdom, / But a child who get his own way brings shame to his mother." Reproof is verbal instruction about what is right and particularly what is wrong.

"Spare the rod and spoil the child" is not in the Bible. The Bible endorses physical correction to the point of delivering a child from death or hell (Proverbs 23:13-14). Discipline should always be done in love. I confess that there were times when I reacted to my children's disobedience rashly. I am ashamed that I did not model more of our heavenly Father's discipline. Corporal punishment must be done under control, and it should be commensurate to the act of disobedience. Discipline must be consistent (Proverbs 13:24). It takes work to direct children toward walking with God.

Samson, Absalom, Eli's sons, and others mentioned in the Bible failed to learn at home. Some parents say, "If I discipline, I will lose my child." The Bible says if you do not discipline you will lose your child. Obviously, it is best to start when children are young. If you start discipline when they are in their teen years, it is probably too late for corporal punishment. But it is never too late to teach discipline. The breakdown in our culture can be laid at the feet of the lack of discipline in the home. Respect for authority, submission to authority, and a sense of justice regarding wrongdoing are missing when there is no discipline.

> *It is never too late to teach discipline. The breakdown in our culture can be laid at the feet of the lack of discipline in the home.*

God's standard is love without compromise. God is holy; God is grace. Because of Jesus, He can be both. The story of the prodigal son in Luke 15 shows how the Father is ready to forgive. He will extend grace if we come back to Him. Jesus gives us a picture in this story of a father's love for a wayward son: "His father saw him and felt compassion for him, and ran and embraced him and kissed him" (verse 20). One of the most endearing moments in my parenting was when I stopped being an enforcer of the law and extended grace. Without compromising biblical truth I was able to say I love you. We are never more like Jesus than when we forgive. Regardless how egregious an act a child may have done, he or she is to be received just as we were received by our heavenly Father.

Someone is going to instill values in your child's mind. "Give me four years to teach the children and the seed I have sown will never be uprooted" is a quote that has been attributed to Vladimir Lenin. Lenin, the cruel ruler of communist Russia, knew that the future of his dominance would be the control of young minds. Young minds are impressionable. God intended that parents be the ones to teach their children.

The primary calling of believing parents is to point their children to Jesus, and it is their high, holy obligation. I have had parents tell how they brought their children to church but now the children deny the truth. People do not get saved by a holy osmosis system. Sitting in a church or going to a children's Bible class is no substitute for parental guidance in spiritual truth. Point your children to Jesus. Acts 16:30-33 gives a picture of household salvation. "And after he brought them out, he said, 'Sirs, what must I do to be saved?' They said, 'Believe in the Lord Jesus, and you will be saved, you and your household.' And they spoke the word of the Lord to him together with all who were in his house. And he took them that very hour of the night and washed their wounds, and immediately he was baptized, he and all his household."

Paul and Silas had been whipped by the authorities for preaching the gospel. They were imprisoned, but an earthquake freed them. The jailer feared for his life because if the prisoners escaped he would have been put to death. He had heard Paul and Silas singing and praying. He knew he had a spiritual need, and he wanted to know how he could have what they had. The promise Paul and Silas gave to the jailer about household salvation was still received individually; each member of the jailer's household had to believe on the Lord Jesus. The jailer simply exposed them to the gospel. As believing parents our desire is to see our children come know Jesus. We must expose them in our homes to the gospel. This most sacred of duties cannot be left up to the pastor, church staff, or a teacher.

Parents are to influence moral and emotional decisions with everyday activities and absolutes in conduct. Solomon reflected on his childhood in Proverbs 4:1-5:

Hear, O sons, the instruction of a father,
And give attention that you may gain understanding,
For I give you sound teaching;
Do not abandon my instruction.
When I was a son to my father,
Tender and the only son in the sight of my mother,
Then he taught me and said to me,
"Let your heart hold fast my words;
Keep my commandments and live;
Acquire wisdom! Acquire understanding!
Do not forget, nor turn away from the words of my mouth."

Parents are to craft the mind, heart, and soul of their children to reflect God's will. I have had parents tell me they do not want to interfere with their children's spiritual or moral decision-making. My response to them is, "Do you impose your ideas of hygiene on them by making them take baths and brush their teeth?" My follow-up, at least in my mind, is "What kind of system of belief do you have that is so lackluster that you don't want to pass it on to your children?" The psalmist describes children as arrows (127:4). Arrows when shot by an archer have an intended target. Parents are to aim their children with a purpose to accomplish much for the glory of God.

A common practice in many churches is to have a baby dedication. Actually, this is a misnomer. The parents are the ones who are being dedicated. They are the ones who must accept the challenge to raise their children in the Lord. I have included a simple ceremony that I have used in dedicating parents to the awesome joy of raising kids.

PARENT/BABY DEDICATION

Introduction: Recognizing that children are a gift from the Lord, and that you have been entrusted with the care of an eternal soul, I am asking you pledge before this congregation and the Lord Jesus Himself your dedication.

Pledge:

I will have a Christlike attitude. I will honor my life mate by having Ephesians 5 as the standard for my home. I will seek to show love and grace to those in my family.

I will live my life in an exemplary manner. I will not knowingly use any substance that would harm my body or others. I will only engage in wholesome entertainment as a family or individual. My life will be lived for Christ before my child.

I will study the Word of God as a family. I will pray daily together as a family. I will attend worship regularly. I will seek to win my child to Christ.

All that I pledge to do is by the power of the Holy Spirit. I commit my child to God. I will pray daily for him (her) until I leave this life to see Jesus.

Scripture Reading:
Psalm 127:1a, 3-5

Dedicatory Prayer

FOR FURTHER STUDY AND DISCUSSION

1. In a society that tells us not to hug and kiss our kids when they reach those teen years, how can we help our families value appropriate affection in the home?

2. In what ways can church workers and leaders love on kids in their care appropriately yet with an understanding of safety and security?

3. What are some ways we can encourage our parents to discipline their kids well when biblical discipline is no longer accepted in our culture?

4. Are you encouraging parents to help their families take faith home? If so, how?

5. Map out some ways to refocus baby dedication to help parents understand their responsibility to raise their children to love God as well as the congregation's responsibility to hold them to that commitment.

CHAPTER 6

MARRIAGE

UNTIL DEATH DO WE PART

have had the privilege of performing the marriage ceremony for all three of our children. Each ceremony was different. Our oldest wanted a destination wedding. So we were in a room overlooking Niagara Falls. Although a Canadian "Marrying Sam" signed the documents, I led in the vows. Our younger daughter wanted a Cinderella wedding. It was High Church. She had attendants, several music pieces, and a large reception. Our son's wife wanted a simple, small wedding. They chose a unique venue near our home. It was lovely. All of the wedding ceremonies had a common statement in my instructions. I explained to them that, for the Christian, the word *divorce* was eradicated from their vocabulary. I told them divorce was not an option. My wife and I pray daily for our adult children. We know the assurance of that request remaining true is dependent on the couples themselves. They must be committed on a daily basis to keep their marriage anchored on the Rock and to keep it from going on the rocks.

In spite of everyone's best efforts, divorce happens to Christians and non-Christians. For years people have been told that Christians divorce at or above the same rate as unbelievers. This is simply not true. Here is an excerpt from *Psychology Today* about the myth that 50 percent of marriages end in divorce:

> It used to be, but overall divorce rates have been falling for a few decades. The truth is, the average couple getting married today has more like a *75 percent* chance of *staying* married. That means that only about 1 in 4 recent marriages are likely to end in divorce.
>
> Second, the likelihood of divorce isn't the same for all couples. For some, the chance of a divorce is very slim, while for others, the chance of divorce is actually greater than 50 percent—for example, higher-order marriages have a higher divorce rates than we once attributed to all marriages. In other words, if you are entering into a second or third marriage, you face an approximately 75 percent chance of getting divorced, or possibly higher. Why is this? There are likely many possible reasons: If you have divorced before, you are statistically more likely to do it again. If your partner has also divorced before, then (as you might imagine) your joint risk of divorce is even higher. Studies show that those who consider divorce a viable option are more likely to choose it when times get tough. In addition, those who have previously divorced have ex-husbands and/or ex-wives, and often children from those earlier marriages in their circle. These additional people, and the issues they bring with them, can be "baggage" that puts a strain on a new relationship.
>
> Finally, there are many factors that influence a couple's chance of getting a divorce, so for any one couple to blindly accept that the 50/50 probability applies to them is a misleading over-simplification that could potentially

become disruptive. Going into a life-long commitment with the idea that you only have a 50/50 chance of staying together can be damaging. If you only truly *commit* half of yourself, it isn't likely to work. If you believe in your heart that the chances of success are a coin-flip, you might walk away when things get tough instead of putting in the work necessary for a successful marriage. Most important is what we call the *self-fulfilling prophesy* [sic]. Simply put, if you believe that your chances of failing are high, then you are likely to see signs that you are "failing" more readily, and then use those signs as a confirmation that you are in fact failing. (This is also known as the confirmation bias.) In this case, you may actually be sabotaging your marriage.[1]

If you Google the question about Christian divorce rates, you will find the revealing truth that people of faith do as well or better than the secular. Couples who have regular religious involvement increase their success rate exponentially. This is encouraging news, but divorce does happen to followers of Jesus Christ. What does the Bible say about divorce and remarriage?

Let's start with Jesus. He was confronted by the strict religious leaders of his day, the Pharisees. They asked if it was permissible before God for a man to divorce his wife for any reason. At the time of Jesus' teachings, women had virtually no rights in the Jewish religious system. A man could divorce his wife with impunity. Jesus begins a discourse on marriage.

And He answered and said, "Have you not read that He who created them from the beginning made them male and female, and said, 'for this cause a man shall leave his father and mother and be joined to his wife, and the two shall become one flesh'? So, they are no longer two, but one flesh. What therefore God has joined together, let no man separate." (Matthew 19:4-6)

These few short sentences are packed with an exhaustive number of theological and practical truths. Jesus affirmed gender assignment. There is no third or more gender identification. He put his stamp of approval on marriage being between one man and one woman. Although the Old Testament gives accounts of faithful believers having more than one wife, Jesus underscores God's ideal of one man for one woman for life. Jesus' "one flesh" comment imports the mystical connection two people have, not just through sexual intercourse, but in sharing life together as one unit. He reiterated that this union is permanent until death. This is God's grand plan for every marriage.

The Pharisees would not let go of their exploitation of women without a fight. They pointed back to a provision made in the Old Testament law that allowed for divorce. Jesus clarified the interpretation of the passage of Scripture in verses 8-9: "Because of your hardness of heart Moses permitted you to divorce your wives; but from the beginning it has not been this way. And I say to you, whoever divorces his wife, except for immorality, and marries another commits adultery."

Jesus closed the Pharisees' loopholes. He said sexual indiscretion should be the only reason for divorce and remarriage. Jesus' explanation to the Pharisees addressed the fundamental issue of divorce and remarriage for any reason. God has more to say on this matter.

Jesus underscored God's ideal of one man for one woman for life.

The apostle Paul, under the inspiration of the Holy Spirit, addressed this difficult subject. The Corinthian church had many problems. They had corresponded with Paul about marital situations. Apparently, they were seeing people accept Jesus as Savior and then leave their unbelieving spouse.

Some people were living together without being married. There was even a case of a man living with his stepmother. The Corinthians were some of the most dysfunctional Christians in apostolic times. God sent directions for their lives that remain for us today. In particular, postmarital relationships were addressed.

> But to the married I give instructions, not I, but the Lord, that the wife should not leave her husband (but if she does leave, she must remain unmarried, or else be reconciled to her husband), and that the husband should not divorce his wife.
>
> But to the rest I say, not the Lord, that if any brother has a wife who is an unbeliever, and she consents to live with him, he must not divorce her. And a woman who has an unbelieving husband, and he consents to live with her, she must not send her husband away. For the unbelieving husband is sanctified through his wife, and the unbelieving wife is sanctified through her believing husband; for otherwise your children are unclean, but now they are holy. Yet if the unbelieving one leaves, let him leave; the brother or the sister is not under bondage in such cases, but God has called us to peace. For how do you know, O wife, whether you will save your husband? Or how do you know, O husband whether you will save your wife? (1 Corinthians 7:10-16)

In answer to the Corinthians' questions, Paul distinguished what he was saying under the inspiration of the Holy Spirit in addition to Jesus' original statements. Paul's directives were not contradictory to Jesus' words but rather expanding on the subject of divorce.

It appears that a woman would have the right to leave her husband, but she was instructed to not remarry. She was told to be ready for reconciliation to her husband. The husband was not to cause his wife to leave. Relative to believers married to unbelievers, they were to stay together; the believer would have the opportunity to be a witness in the home. The children would benefit spiritually from the saved person's presence.

Some interpretations of verse 15 allow for an extra reason for divorce and remarriage. If an unbeliever deserted the believing spouse, the language in the verse indicates that the believer would be free to remarry. Paul uses similar language in Romans 7:2-3 when he is teaching about being free from the law. He says a man and woman are bound together until death. It seems that the bonds of marriage are dissolved if the unbeliever deserts the believer. This could open the door for another reason for divorce and remarriage.

Right or wrong, divorce happens. Malachi 2:16 reads, "'For I hate divorce' says the LORD, the God of Israel." God hates divorce, but he loves people. While divorce is devastating, it is not the unpardonable sin. God will forgive.

God called Israel his wife, but she was unfaithful to Him. God used the prophet Hosea as an example of extreme love. Hosea's attempt at reconciliation went beyond what most would ever try. Some work at reconciliation to the extreme. Fortunately, this is the type of love God exhibits for us. We wander away to other spiritual lovers, but He loves us back to himself. When reconciliation is not possible in a broken marriage, at least the healing of God's love can be present in everyone's life.

Divorce is the severing of two into separate entities. It is one of the harshest words in the English language when it is spoken about marriage.

In 1 Corinthians 7:15, God calls us to peace. Although the pain of betrayal may sting, believers are to find their way to peace through a walk with Jesus. The valley of divorce may be long and hard, but God will be your guide to peace.

These steps will help you begin the journey:

1. Be honest with God about sin and mistakes.
2. Decide you will deal with your situation from Scripture.
3. Commit your life to the lordship of Jesus Christ.
4. Seek godly counsel.
5. Stay in the fellowship of God's people.

---

1 Renée Peltz Dennison PhD., "Do Half of All Marriages Really End in Divorce?" *Heart of the Matter* (blog), *Psychology Today*, April 24, 2017, https://www.psychologytoday .com/us/blog/heart-the-matter/201704/do-half-all-marriages-really-end-in-divorce.

FOR FURTHER STUDY AND DISCUSSION

1. Why is the institution of marriage between a woman and a man such an important thing?

2. How can you encourage your couples to begin praying together?

3. Do you have divorce in your family? How do you feel it has affected you and your family?

4. The best way to keep from ever considering divorce is to make sure it is never an option. What are some things that you must do regularly to ensure this truth in your home and in the church?

5. How can your church minister to those who find
   themselves in a marriage with someone who does not
   believe in Jesus? What must we encourage them to do?

CHAPTER 7

SENIOR ADULTS

FOURTH-QUARTER LIVING

My son and I have talked about doing a little business venture together. He was explaining to me that in twenty years the investments would begin to really pay off. I told him I am in the fourth quarter of the game of life. I do not have twenty years to wait on the investment. I know I have already won the game. I intend to keep throwing the ball and running up the score until the final gun sounds. But I have to be intentional about the time I have left.

Baby boomers (those born in the years 1946–1964) resist identifying with old age. Generally they are more active than any preceding senior generation. People are living longer with a higher quality of enjoyment. Boomers remember growing up in church as children. The boomers may be the last generation with a church memory unless there is a spiritual awakening in the American culture. The boomers had a close brush with a spiritual awakening in the 1970s. The Jesus Movement brought many people into God's kingdom. Nothing like that ingathering of youth and young adults has been seen since. It may be the boomers will be called upon in their later days to lead a rising generation to the Lord Jesus Christ.

Scriptures are ample that show the role of older believers. Titus 2:1-5 gives instructions to the older men and women about their contribution in shaping the future. Paul addressed the issues of seniors serving in the church. He wanted to underscore that a real salvation experience produces a relational ministry to others. He gave direction about order in the home and church. Titus was assigned to the church on the island of Crete. The people of Crete were challenged to adapt their lifestyles to the teaching of Scripture. Most believers have the concept of going to church rather than *being* the church. As we mature spiritually, and with age, we have more to offer others along life's way. We show our salvation experience by right relationships and living out our faith.

Paul underscored that a real salvation experience produces a relational ministry to others.

Paul pointed out that sound doctrine produces godly living (Titus 2:1). The Bible gives us the design for virtually every area of life. Young and old, male and female, are instructed about the way they can serve the Lord. The Bible is our infallible guidebook for life.

Senior men are to provide true leadership in attitude and conduct. Titus 2:2 says, "Older men are to be temperate, dignified, sensible, sound in the faith, in love, in perseverance."

Being temperate means not going to extremes in any area of life. Balance is the ideal for all believers. A dignified lifestyle is one of holiness. It is not just about proper manners or decorum; this is a dignity that points upward to the Lord's high holiness. Holiness is possible through the power of the indwelling Spirit. The charge to be sensible is similar to being temperate. Older men should have acquired enough life experiences to enable them to avoid rash actions. Most of us learn in the school of hard knocks. It is foolish to live through life experiences and not be better for them. Wisdom that comes from difficult decisions can help younger believers avoid pitfalls.

Being sound in the faith means to know what you believe. Actually it involves pouring true doctrine into others. Clear articulation of the faith, coupled with consistent living, becomes a value to those with a teachable spirit. The faith is a system of doctrines and truths found in the scriptures. What we believe about the nature of Scripture, the person of Christ, salvation, and practical applications of biblical facts shapes our lives. These truths are what older men are to transmit to younger men.

True love toward particularly younger mentees requires trust, openness, and genuine care for those who need it most. We are to love people where they are in order to get them to where they need to be. Love is not compromise of biblical truth. Real love is not syrupy sentimentalism. Love is a bedrock conviction about biblical truth that is shared in a kind, gracious manner.

The Greek word translated "perseverance" or "patience" is *hupomone*. This word is made of two words that mean to "abide under." When older men remain faithful, year after year, through suffering or difficult circumstances, they will earn the respect of those who have been watching. Patience is not a natural attribute of any age. The older we get, the more difficult patience becomes. Only a believer yielded up to the Holy Spirit can exemplify these qualities.

As a young pastor I became pastor of a church with a seventy-nine-year-old chairman of deacons. He was the only chairman of deacons the church had ever had. He could have greatly hindered my ministry. Instead he was the most important layman mentor in my ministry. He exhibited the characteristics of a Spirit-controlled man. He was able to shepherd through leadership of the church evangelistic outreach efforts, building programs, and other innovative activities. Without his help I would not have been able to get ministries accomplished without tremendous difficulty. My godly deacon planted many trees that he never sat under the shade. I am still enjoying the fruits of his life. I want to be that kind of senior leader.

Senior ladies have a tremendous calling as described in Titus 2:3-5. "Older women likewise are to be reverent in their behavior, not malicious gossips nor enslaved to much wine, teaching what is good. That they may encourage the young women to love their husbands, to love their children, to be sensible, pure, workers at home, kind, being subject to their own husbands, that the word of God will not be dishonored."

Older women are to instill in the younger women a pattern of godliness that magnifies the message of the Lord Jesus Christ. The senior ladies were warned about being gossips. The Greek word for "gossips" is *diablos*, from which we get the word "devil." This is an indication of the destructive power of the improper use of the tongue.

Alcohol use in social settings has not changed much through the centuries. Neither has the heartbreak of alcohol. Some make the argument that the phrase "nor enslaved to much wine" provides an open door for alcoholic consumption by believers. While some Christians insist on exercising their liberty to imbibe alcoholic beverages, wisdom dictates abstinence. Even if a person believes that alcohol use as a beverage may be permissible for the believer, such an approach allows the unnecessary potential for alcohol's devastating effects.

Older ladies are to teach younger women about life in the home. Romance had little to do with most marital relationships in the first century. As followers of Jesus the younger women were to learn how to love their husbands. Love is sometimes an acquired action. Love is a decision after the emotions cool. Sensual love does not have to dissipate with the years; but even if it does, love remains an act of the will.

It would be reasonable to think a mother would know how to love her children. Yet family planning was not discussed in New Testament times. Oftentimes, children were produced to be an economic asset. Working in an agrarian society required a lot of workers. These mothers were to do more than provide food for their children; they were expected to be the prime teachers of spiritual truth to the young. A mother's loving her children would cause a greater desire to care for their spiritual needs.

Women have a myriad of obligations. Most work outside the home, and career commitments can crowd into family life. Motherhood is a high calling. Love is best exemplified by making the family the priority above all other endeavors.

Young women were to be taught discretion. Purity is an outgrowth of a holy lifestyle. Modesty becomes women. Strange as it may seem, evangelical Christians and liberal, radical feminists agree that women should not be sex objects. Even in our politically incorrect environment consensus can be reached that women should not be devalued. The Christian takes purity to a proper conclusion to say women are to honor the Lord Jesus with their bodies. First-century culture treated women as property, but Jesus and the New Testament writers elevated women's status to one of honor.

Complementarianism is clear in Titus 2:5. While women are equal with men in their standing before God (Galatians 3:28), their function is different. A clear witness of the gospel before a watching world depends on husbands and wives having the right relationship with one another. There is no stronger witness to those who need Jesus than a home that projects a gospel witness in the marriage relationship.

The Bible cites abundant examples of senior saints who were used of God. Moses is one of the most prominent. He began his ministry around the age of eighty. While few people live to be 120 as Moses did, it is a fact that he came into his own in the last fourth of his life. To approximate Moses' years of effectiveness, a person today would start at about fifty-five years of age. Caleb claimed his inheritance in the promised land at eighty-five. He is an example of God's sustaining power for the task He gives you.

In the New Testament when Jesus appeared at the temple as a baby he was greeted by two fourth-quarter saints. We can make logical conjecture that Simeon was advanced in age, since God had promised Simeon he would live to see the Messiah. Anna was praying and worshipping on a daily basis at the temple. She was about one hundred years of age. Both Simeon and Anna testified of the saving power of Jesus. Timothy was influenced in the faith by his grandmother and mother. Paul called himself the "aged" meaning that he was getting up in years (Philemon 9). Culminating the writing of inspired Scripture, John the Beloved was almost one hundred when he penned Revelation. The retirement plan for the child of God is out of this world. We are never to end our service to the Lord this side of our last breath.

Paul, concluding his instructions about age-related interaction, wrote to Titus that he based every ministry and motivation on the salvation relationship with Jesus Christ. Because of Jesus we have a life of purpose and direction. Titus 2:11-15 reads:

> For the grace of God has appeared, bringing salvation to all men, instructing us to deny ungodliness and worldly desires and to live sensibly, righteously and godly in the present age, looking for the blessed hope and the appearing of the glory of our great God and Savior, Christ Jesus, who gave Himself for us to redeem us from every lawless deed, and to purify for Himself a people for His own possession, zealous for good deeds.
>
> These things speak and exhort and reprove with all authority. Let no one disregard you.

A synopsis of these verses is expressed in these closing remarks. The presence of His grace has universal appeal. Those who receive grace have the power to live for Jesus. If we have experienced His grace we will desire to see Him! Saving grace is purifying grace— it cleans us up. Real life comes as a result of living according to biblical principles.

Paul told Titus to model service and teach truth. For those who are in the fourth quarter, it is time to put forth our best effort. Living according to biblical principles will give us the best life. You cannot do better than God's best. As we follow the Lord Jesus, our lives will become an evident witness of His grace. Keep throwing the ball! Keep running up the score until the gun sounds!

FOR FURTHER STUDY AND DISCUSSION

1. How are older men and women to model Christian character to the next generations?

2. Why is displaying dignity and decorum important for the mature man?

3. As a church, find ways to share the spiritual stories of the senior adults in the church.

4. The coming generations are very different than the boomers. How can they find common ground to develop mentor relationships in the church?

5. How can the church empower and engage fourth-quarter saints in the church? Develop some specific ideas.

6. Look for ways to encourage the mature persons in the church to seek out younger believers in whom to invest.

CHAPTER 8

SINGLENESS

ONE IS NOT THE LONELIEST NUMBER

When I was a teenager, there was a popular song with the title "One." The first line opens with these words, "One is the loneliest number that you'll ever do."[1] It was conveying a message about a guy who was unable to connect with another. For Christian singles, one does not have to be the loneliest number.

> Now concerning the things about which you wrote, it is good for a man not to touch a woman. But because of immoralities, each man is to have his own wife, and each woman is to have her own husband . . . But this I say by way of concession, not of command. Yet I wish that all men were even as I myself am. However, each man has his own gift from God, one in this manner, and another in that.

But I say to the unmarried and to widows that it is good for them if they remain even as I. But if they do not have self-control, let them marry; for it is better to marry than to burn with passion.

Only, as the Lord has assigned to each one, as God has called each, in this manner let him walk. And thus I direct in all the churches. (1 Corinthians 7:1-2, 6-9, 17)

People are waiting longer to get married than in recent history. Delaying marriage has both positive and negative repercussions. Some of the positives include completing a degree, serving in the military, and starting a career or volunteering full-time in charitable work. Some of the negatives are loneliness, feeling left out, or discrimination. How are people to know if marriage is for them? How is a person to know if he or she is to stay single? Some of those questions and others are answered in Paul's reply to a troubled church.

> "As the Lord has assigned to each one, as God has called each, in this manner let him walk."
> (1 Corinthians 7:17)

First Corinthians 7 is one of the best passages for looking at singleness, marriage and the not yet married. The church had doctrinal error. The church had sinful practices. Some in the church wanted to get their walk with the Lord right, and they wrote the apostle Paul inquiring about God's will for their lives. They touched upon marital relationships, sexual mores, and singleness. Paul responded by giving the church clear direction about these subjects.

Dating is a practice developed in the Western culture. The Bible does not say much about long courtships. There is one exception. Jacob paid dearly for his love of Rachel (Genesis 29). He served seven years as a worker for his father-in-law Laban to gain her hand. Laban tricked Jacob by sending Rachel's sister Leah into the honeymoon suite. Eventually, Jacob served Laban another seven years for Rachel. He ended up with a tough taskmaster in Laban and too many wives.

Customs change, but God's standards never change. "It is good for a man not to touch a woman" (1 Corinthians 7:1). This is euphemistic language for refraining from sexual activity before marriage. Purity prior to marriage is God's ideal. Both parties should remain virgins until they are united in marriage. Abstinence from sexual activity is God's design for the single person. Sadly, many singles in today's culture see no negatives in having sexual activity before marriage. Cohabitation has become an acceptable practice. Even Christians dismiss the plain teachings of Scripture when it comes to sexual purity. You would have to have your head buried in the sand to think that unmarried people are not having sexual intercourse.

The undeniable truth is that men and women are having sex at a younger age. All the while, the millennial generation is marrying at a later age. Single adults who are not sexually active are subject to being the butt of jokes. Society's standards have changed to the point that those who abstain from sex before marriage are the odd ones. Sex has become socially acceptable because of self-gratification. In verse 9, Paul counsels that if a couple cannot contain their sexual desires, it would be better for them to marry.

In 1 Corinthians 7:6-8, Paul tells the unmarried that he is speaking from his personal perspective. The words are inspired from God, but Paul is saying it is not God's command for everyone to be single. Paul then goes on to say he thinks it is best to be single. He recognized that singleness was a gift, and he told the unmarried people in the church that he was single. He considered himself fulfilled in his singleness. Some well-meaning people counsel singles that if they stay faithful to God, He will bring their lifemate to them. Marriage may not be God's plan for everyone. It is God's plan to point more to Christ. Knowing Jesus in an intimate walk is the only desire that will not lead to disappointment, whether married or single. We are called to know Him and make Him known.

Jesus' mission from the Father called for Him to have a different approach to singleness. Jesus was all God and all man. Although tempted in all areas as we are, Jesus never sinned (Hebrews 4:15). His unique calling was to live a perfect life in order to die on the cross to pay for our sins. His singleness was ordained of the Father.

Jesus addressed singleness in an answer to a question from His disciples. They heard Jesus teach on marriage and divorce. Some of the disciples deduced that it would be better to never marry than to marry and divorce. Jesus replied to them from a different perspective.

> But He said to them, "Not all men can accept this statement, but only those to whom it has been given. For there are eunuchs who were born that way from their mother's womb; and there are eunuchs who were made eunuchs by men; and there are also eunuchs who made themselves eunuchs for the sake of the kingdom of heaven. He who is able to accept this, let him accept it." (Matthew 19:11-12)

Jesus was not advocating for a particular lifestyle. He was simply conveying the information that there are different reasons people are celibate. People who do not marry may have no desire to do so. Others may have suffered some injury. Remaining celibate for the advance of the gospel is a choice some will make.

One of the godliest men I have known was Percy Ray. Percy Ray pastored Myrtle Baptist Church in Myrtle, Mississippi for almost a half century. He founded a camp called Camp Zion that literally drew thousands into the rural countryside to hear the preaching of God's Word. Brother Percy, as he was affectionately called, said the purpose of the camp was threefold: to get a working knowledge of the Word of God; to better understand the work of the Holy Spirit in the life of the believer; and to pray for revival in Baptist churches. Brother Percy and R. G. Lee, who was the pastor of Bellevue Baptist Church in Memphis, Tennessee, were close friends. Dr. Lee would later become president of the Southern Baptist Convention. The story is told that Brother Percy and Dr. Lee's daughter became engaged. One night the couple prayed about their marriage at a church altar. Brother Percy prayed all night long. When he looked up the next morning, his fiancé was gone. They never got married. Brother Percy remained single the rest of his life. He answered a call to singleness that brought many sons and daughters into the family of God.

Paul concluded his comments on celibacy to the Corinthians by giving guidelines pertaining to various situations (1 Corinthians 7:25-40). There was no doubt in Paul's mind that he was writing inspired words.

You may or may not have a call to singleness. The direction God gives to all of us is to seek to make His name great (Matthew 6:33). When we do that we will be fulfilled regardless of our marital status.

A very narrow area of family life is singleness as a young widow. This subject is addressed in 1 Timothy 5:3-16. During Paul's day, a woman who lost her husband to death could very well be destitute. She might become desperate. There was no social safety net. Apparently some of the younger widows began to practice immorality. Others left the walk of faith. Paul gave instructions to the church about the treatment of widows. He called for the extended family to care for widows both young and old.

The Old Testament gives numerous insight to the care for widows (Deuteronomy 10:18; 14:29; 24:17; Psalm 94:6; Isaiah 1:17; Malachi 3:5). The government should not be responsible to care for those who are in need. The relatives were the first caregivers; then the church was to step up (1 Timothy 5:3-4, 6-8).

The qualifications for assistance are listed: the widow must be without other means of support, a believer, at least sixty years of age, have a good marriage record, and have participated in good works toward other believers (verses 5, 9-10). The early church had an official list of acceptable recipients of aid. Indications were that the younger widows had a tendency to take the financial support, and then marry, usually an unbeliever (verses 11-13, 15).

The twenty-first century provides different challenges to young widows. Yet the church is to come alongside them. Compassion for their loss is the first expression. Helping them get back to a place of stability is second. In all of this, the church is to walk through this valley with her to make it a spiritually strengthening journey. Principles of Scripture apply to widowers as well. When there is loss of a spouse, the people of God are to rally to the grieving. Knowing whether marriage or singleness is God's future plan will develop through the healing process.

Singleness has the same call to a relationship as in any other season in life. Everyone is called to a relationship with Jesus. Once a person knows Jesus as Lord and Savior there is an unbroken relationship. This relationship can grow deeper. As we walk with Jesus daily, He can bring clarity to our lives. Whether single or married, as long as we are in His will, we are never alone.

1 Harry Nilsson, *One* (Van Nuys, CA: Alfred Publishing Co. Inc., 1968), www.musicnotes.com.

FOR FURTHER STUDY AND DISCUSSION

1. How are single adults viewed in our churches?

2. In a culture where sexual abstinence is mocked, how do we help today's singles maintain purity?

3. How can we find places of leadership in our churches for those who feel called to singleness?

4. How can married couples in your church encourage the single adults to value and understand God's purpose in marriage?

5. As a church how can we do a better job of caring for the widows?

CHAPTER 9

WHAT ABOUT EVERYONE ELSE?

COUPLES WITHOUT CHILDREN

Perhaps one of the most difficult topics to cover in a book on the family is a childless couple. There are several examples in Scripture of couples who wanted children but were unable to have them. Some people have chosen not to have children. Regardless of the scenario, Mother's Day and Father's Day can be hard for a childless couple.

Similar to a single person, couples without children can give more of themselves to the Lord. They can immerse themselves in ministry. Paul the apostle invested his life in Timothy. Barnabas was a mentor to Mark. Anecdotally, I have observed how God used two couples to pour into the lives of others. Robert Holmes was a church planter, soul-winner, pastor, and warrior for the inerrancy of Scripture. He and his wife had no children, but he was a spiritual father to me and many others. My dad's brother was exposed to radiation during World War II, and it caused him to be infertile. He and his wife treated me as a son. My life and my children are beneficiaries of their love and generosity.

Modern science has enabled couples who were previously unable to have children to welcome babies into their home. Some couples who cannot have biological children choose adoption. Other couples with children add to their number through adoption. My wife was adopted. She was blessed by the woman who did not bear her but who helped bring her to Christ. Adoption is a beautiful picture of the gospel; we have been adopted in Christ (Romans 8:15). *The Baptist Faith and Message* Article XVIII on the family says a family "is composed of persons related to one another by marriage, blood, or adoption."[1] While some who are treated as family never get legally adopted, it is a testimony of God's grace when we embrace others into our lives.

> *Similar to a single person, couples without children can give more of themselves to the Lord.*

A childless couple can be a power producer of spiritual prodigy. Ultimately, our family is broader than those we biologically produce.

ADULT CHILDREN

Adult children are waiting longer to leave home. Books have been written about parents learning how to let an emerging adult child go. Sometimes you let them go and they come back! Adult children living in their parents' basement and spending their time blogging while in their pajamas is the caricature of male millennials. Initiative and responsibility has to be taught at an early age. Spiritual truth will prompt a person to pursue God's will for his or her life.

What is a parent to do with wayward adult children? Keep the communication lines open, and set a regular time to talk. This is a crucial ingredient in keeping them exposed to the Word of God. Build them up where you can, and accentuate the positive in their lives. Verbalize to them that they will always be important to you. Tell them that they will never get beyond your love. Kids never grow up as it relates to needing the assurance of a parent's love. There are no easy answers. There are no guarantees. But there is hope. Find forgiveness for your own failures, then press on following Jesus.

There comes a point when you can do no more for your children. Maybe you failed to provide spiritually during their early years. Maybe you did try to disciple them to Christ, but something has gone amiss in their lives. What does an adult child need? What do the parents need? Adult children need to be reminded of scriptural truth. Proverbs 22:6 speaks to younger children, but adult children are not "old." If a child is still under your roof you can speak truth into his or her life. This is not some legalistic command. It is a loving reminder.

When you have done what you can with your children, once they reach adulthood they must stand before the Lord individually (Romans 14:12). Release them to the Lord. Do not try to control them. As parents continue life with adult children, our most powerful tool is to let Jesus be Lord in our lives first.

In this same vein, some grandparents have had to adopt or rear their grandchildren. A faithful pastor friend and his wife are caring for their grandchildren; one has severe special needs. God's grace and a loving church family can enable people to bear virtually impossible burdens.

CHILDREN WITHOUT BELIEVING PARENTS

Young people who have unbelieving parents sometimes get saved. What are they to do? The apostle Paul told Timothy to be an example of a believer. Timothy was a young preacher, not a child, who had a godly heritage. However, the principles of Paul's charge to Timothy relate to teenagers and children who are in an unbelieving home.

First Timothy 4:12 is a challenge Paul gave to the young preacher, Timothy. It reads, "Let no one look down on your youthfulness, but rather in speech, conduct, love, faith and purity, show yourself an example of those who believe." There are several ways believing children and teens can be a witness in the home. The first way is to live out what you profess. This is difficult for anyone, but by the power of God's Spirit it is possible. What we say and how we act shows what is in our hearts. Stay conscious that Jesus is a party to our interactions with others. Lifestyle change is a strong indicator that Jesus has made you a new person and oftentimes does not go unnoticed by unbelievers.

Second, know the power of love. Love is the birthmark of every believer. Parents need love. Students need love. Only Jesus can help us love properly.

Having faith with a pure heart is the third way a believing child or teen can live for Christ in an unbelieving home. Students have more temptations now than any preceding generation. The electronic traps are deadly in themselves. Faith gives victory over temptation. "So then faith comes by hearing, and hearing by the word of God" (Romans 10:17 NKJV). Immersion in the scriptures gives students the strength to run from temptation. A support group in the church can reinforce the Word. By having the power of the Spirit of God, a student can live a pure life. Without parental support it is difficult for a student, but God will supply others who can be a support system.

Young people have much to contribute to the cause of Christ. Some of the greatest movements of God came through young people. Often it is the older generation that pours cold water on the fires of the Spirit. As a student who is a believer, look to those who encourage you in the faith.

WIVES WITHOUT BELIEVING HUSBANDS

First Peter 3:1-6 applies to the home where a husband is not a believer. Speaking directly to women whose husbands were unbelievers, Peter tells the believing wife that she could be the witness to bring about her husband's salvation. He said it was more than outward acts of obedience but a holy lifestyle before God with a sweet spirit that would make the difference. A woman's godly behavior is the primary influence on unbelieving husbands. The passage reads:

> In the same way, you wives, be submissive to your own husbands so that even if any of them are disobedient to the word, they may be won without a word by the behavior of their wives, as they observe your chaste and respectful behavior. Your adornment must not be merely external—braiding the hair, and wearing gold jewelry, or putting on dresses; but let it be the hidden person of the heart, with the imperishable quality of a gentle and quiet spirit, which is precious in the sight of God. For this way in former times the holy women also, who hoped in God, used to adorn themselves, being submissive to the own husbands; just as Sarah obeyed Abraham, calling him lord, and you have become her children if you do what is right without being frightened by any fear.

Although the text speaks about submission "in the same way" (verse 1) as the preceding examples of a slave to a master or a citizen to the government, nowhere does the New Testament teach that women are inferior to men. Women are seen as coheirs of eternal life with their husbands. Throughout the New Testament women were elevated from a low cultural position to one of equality. Submission of wives is a theological truth illustrating the relationship of Christ and the church. The apostle Paul lays out this distinction in Ephesians 5:22-33. The New Testament teaches that the submission of wives to their husbands is a mirror to the church's submission to Jesus.

Outward sex appeal will not convince the unbelieving husband to trust Christ. Staying attentive to the needs of our spouses is part of honoring Christ. Every couple should keep the "honey in the honeymoon." Though the outward appearance may fade, inward beauty lasts a lifetime.

The phrase "hoped in God" meant the women were to submit not because their husbands were superior to them but because the women were confident that God would reward their obedience. Peter used the patriarchs' wives as examples of godly submission. Sarah was the example named in this passage. Her trust in God empowered her to submit to her husband. Sarah put her faith in God even when Abraham's directives placed her in unfavorable conditions (Genesis 12 and 20). God held Abraham accountable and blessed Sarah for her obedience.

Living a faithful, Christian life gives a woman the greatest possibility of leading her unsaved husband to Christ. As in all instances of submission, there are limits. Should there be a physical attack or a threatening environment, the wife should remove herself from harm and report the abusive activity. Absolute submission is not inferred in Scripture. If a husband requires a wife to violate biblical truth or follow another faith system, then the wife should disobey. First-century women were expected to take the religion of their husbands. Peter was introducing a socially radical idea—Jesus always comes first.

---

1 "The Family," Article XVIII, *The Baptist Faith and Message*, Southern Baptist Convention, accessed May 3, 2018, http://www.sbc.net/bfm2000/bfm2000.asp.

FOR FURTHER STUDY AND DISCUSSION

1. What are some ways your church can be sensitive to couples who are unable to have children?

2. How is your church engaging the local community through fostering and adoption?

3. List some ways that parents can build responsibility and initiative into their children to prepare them for adulthood.

4. How can you help a family that needs to communicate some tough love to their adult children?

5. In what ways can churches engage families where one or both parents are not believers?

6. Think of some ways your church can provide for those who are married to a spouse who is not a believer.

CONCLUSION

Building biblical families is a construction zone. There are dangers everywhere, so wear your hard hat! We will complete our work on the family when we leave this life to see Jesus. Until then, the joy is in the journey. We get to see lives transformed by the gospel. Helping young couples as they get started in life is a thrill. Extending grace to those who have suffered divorce makes us more like Jesus. We observe how little children are shaped by the Word of God. It is encouraging when the rising generation of youth assumes their spiritual responsibilities. In all the seasons of life we are blessed to have a part in developing our earthly families. Ultimately, our goal is to exhibit the traits of the family of God.

ABOUT THE AUTHOR

Jim Richards is the executive director of the Southern Baptists of Texas Convention. The SBTC has experienced phenomenal growth both numerically and financially. The Convention has become an important partner for churches in Texas and with the Southern Baptist Convention.

Dr. Richards' education includes two undergraduate degrees, a Master of Divinity from New Orleans Baptist Theological Seminary, and a Doctor of Ministry from Mid-America Baptist Theological Seminary in Memphis. He is a Distinguished Alumnus of both seminaries. The Criswell College in Dallas awarded Dr. Richards the Doctor of Divinity in 2013.

He has authored the books, *Revelation: The Best is Yet to Come, Embracing the Ends of the Earth*, and *Encouraging Words for Difficult Days*, as well as being a contributing author in *The Mission of Today's Church* and *Messages for the Journey*.

Auxano Press
Non-Disposable
Curriculum

- Designed for use in any small group
- Affordable, biblically based, and life oriented
- Choose your own material and stop and start times
- Study the Bible and build a Christian library

Auxano
PRESS

For teaching guides and
additional small group study
materials, or to learn about
other Auxano Press titles, visit
Auxanopress.com.

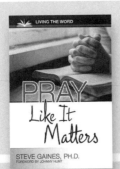

Steve Gaines

Believers who read the New Testament often come away with the conviction that there must be more to following Christ than what they are experiencing. In this Amazon best seller, Steve Gaines points out that the glaring disconnect between modern Christianity and that of the first century is not due to deficiencies in our sermons or our singing. The problem is our praying.

Jim Richards

In today's ever changing culture, Christians need encouragement to respond to the pressures assaulting our faith. In this book believers see how to have victory in Jesus by having a godly attitude while facing trials and challenges.

Steve Gaines

Have you ever been so excited about something that you had to share it with others? That's the way it should be with every Christian. We should be so enthusiastic about the fact that Jesus is our Lord and Savior that we cannot contain the good news. Learn how to politely, scripturally, effectively, and easily share the gospel of Jesus Christ.

For teaching guides and additional small group study materials, or to learn about other Auxano Press titles, visit Auxanopress.com.

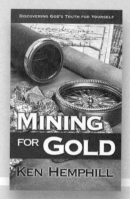